CREATING YOUR AWESOME LIFE

KARIN ABEYTA

BALBOA.PRESS

A DIVISION OF HAY HOUSE

Balboa Press books may be ordered through booksellers or by contacting:

Balboa Press
A Division of Hay House
1663 Liberty Drive
Bloomington, IN 47403
www.balboapress.com
844-682-1282

Print information available on the last page.

ISBN: 979-8-7652-5881-1 (sc)
ISBN: 979-8-7652-5880-4 (e)

Library of Congress Control Number: 2024927140

Balboa Press rev. date: 01/07/2025

CONTENTS

INTRODUCTION

Creating Your Awesome Life

Throughout my life, I have focused on continuous learning, and more recently, I've come across concepts that have profoundly changed me. These ideas showed me how I could shape my life on my own terms and how I have the power to choose my emotions rather than be controlled by them. As I began to learn and apply these concepts, they brought a significant and positive shift to my life. This book shares these insights with kids who are just starting to explore and understand life. I want to give them the tools to feel confident in themselves, no matter what's happening around them, so as they grow up, they can create amazing, fulfilling lives. While some of the concepts in this book have been introduced by other authors, I've included my own reflections, along with space for coloring, journaling, and self-reflection. The authors who've influenced me include Dr. Dawson Church, Brooke Castillo, Louise Hay, Dr. Joe Dispenza, Pam Grout, Dr. Wayne W. Dyer, Jen Sincero, Napoleon Hill, Abraham, Gabrielle Bernstein, and Esther and Jerry Hicks.

LOVE YOURSELF

Love yourself because you are an amazing person and always worth loving. That's simply who you are. You are incredible, and you are awesome. Period. Full stop. That's the whole story. You are amazing, and you are awesome!!

Try writing that a few times here (even if you don't believe it quite yet – practice makes perfect 😊)

I am an incredibly amazing person who is awesome!

_____

_____

_____

_____

_____

_____

_____

_____

There are times when it's easy to believe in your awesomeness—like when you ace a test or get picked for the sports, chess, or math team. In those moments, you feel awesome because you've got this external "proof." But here's the news: drumroll, please! Your awesomeness has nothing to do with any of that. Before you toss this book out the window, think about the flip side. On those rare occasions when you come in second place or make a mistake (gasp!), it might be harder to believe in your awesomeness. But remember, your awesomeness is always there, no matter what's happening in your life.

Just in case you think I'm only saying nice-sounding things, let me tell you about a few things that happened during my junior year of high school. Notice I said things that happened to me, not who I was. In the spring of that year, I interviewed to be a summer counselor at a church camp. I wasn't selected. I applied to join the National Honor Society for the following year. I wasn't chosen. I asked my biggest crush ever to prom. He said no. Then I asked another guy to go to prom. He also said no. By that point, I was ready to crawl under a rock.

But I had a choice: either crawl under that rock and eat worms, or choose to believe that my identity was bigger than what others—people, organizations, employers— were telling me. I chose to believe that my life wasn't over, despite how hard my overly-dramatic high school brain tried to convince me otherwise. I reminded myself that my awesomeness wasn't tied to what was happening around me, but that I was an incredibly amazing person no matter what!

You do this by focusing on who you are, not on what you have, what you look like, what others say about you, or which social group you belong to. Remember, you are an amazing person created by the Universe to be awesome. And that won't change, no matter how many people say no to you for prom.

And more practice: "I am an incredibly amazing person who is awesome!"

up with some examples of ways you can encourage yourself to remember how
ɔme you are, and not eat worms.

_____

_____

_____

_____

_____

_____

_____

_____

_____

_____

_____

_____

_____

_____

_____

_____

Com
awes

1.

2.

3

POSITIVE SELF-TALK

Loving yourself might seem like a silly idea, partly because we often take it for granted. We talk a lot about loving others—or not being too fond of them—but rarely do we stop to think about how we feel about ourselves. So much of our daily life runs on autopilot. We wake up, shower, brush our teeth, and get dressed without much thought, just moving from one task to the next. Sometimes, we treat ourselves the same way: we take ourselves for granted and don't pause to consider how we actually feel about ourselves. But you need to make a habit of loving yourself, always.

_____

_____

_____

_____

_____

_____

_____

_____

Figuring out how we think can be a new concept for many of us. Thinking about thinking feels a bit like trying to remember how to move your feet while walking. So much of our thought process happens automatically, without us even noticing. But when we stop and step back from "ourselves," we might discover a lot of our thoughts aren't all that kind. Some people are their own worst critic without even realizing it. Sometimes, the things you say to yourself are things you'd never dream of saying out loud to anyone else: "I can't believe you messed that up again—how dumb can you be?" "I'm not smart enough to pass that test." "I'll never get that part in the play." You might not even be aware you're "saying" this to yourself, but if you step back and notice what you're thinking, you may want to choose a kinder thought. If you wouldn't say those things to your best friend, don't say them to yourself.

What are some examples of negative things you say to yourself without realizing it?

1)

2)

3)

Side note: If you realize you haven't been kind to yourself, don't beat yourself up over it—that's the opposite of what we're trying to do here. We're all learning and improving, so give yourself credit for that!

If you were talking to your best friend, what would you say to be kind to them?

1)

2)

3)

What would you like to start saying to yourself?

1)

2)

3)

Loving yourself is something you need to practice all the time. This could mean taking a moment for yourself and doing something that makes you feel good. Maybe it's making a cup of tea (or maybe that's just me!). Maybe it's doing a big, long stretch to ground yourself in your body. It could be taking a few deep breaths, or maybe heading to the batting cage to smash some baseballs out of the park. Treat yourself sometimes—you deserve it.

Loving yourself isn't always easy, but it's one of the most important parts of living your awesome life. Practicing self-love doesn't mean you have to think it's okay when you mess up or don't do your best. It means loving yourself regardless. Everyone makes mistakes, and there are things beyond your control. Love yourself anyway. The person you are is amazing—you deserve your own love.

_____

_____

_____

_____

_____

_____

_____

What are some things you can do to remind yourself that you love yourself?

1. Do something you enjoy

2. Treat yourself

3. Give yourself a compliment

4. _____

5. _____

6. _____

_____

_____

_____

_____

_____

_____

_____

_____

_____

_____

LADDER YOUR THOUGHTS HIGHER

I've been telling you how awesome you are and why practicing self-love is so important. But maybe you're feeling like you're at rock bottom, thinking there's no way you'll ever get to a better place with your thoughts. You might be sitting there with thoughts like, "I'm not a good person, and I mess everything up." Moving from that point to a place where you truly love yourself might feel like a huge gap or an enormous cliff. And from where you are, it can seem impossible to get there. The answer? Build yourself a "ladder" to help you climb what looks like that giant cliff. Then, take it one rung at a time.

If you're stuck at the bottom with negative thoughts, you might only be able to take a small step up. Maybe it's an encouraging thought like, "I'm good at taking care of my dog; he always has food," or "I'm always on time for class and don't argue with my teachers." You might think those aren't huge accomplishments, but that's not the point. The point is that they are positive thoughts—a step above that rock-bottom place. And guess what? You just climbed your first rung.

Once you've taken that step, focus on the next one. Your next rung could be something like, "I'm learning to be kinder to myself," or "I'm really organized with my homework." Each rung is a positive step up, and the direction is what matters most. Now that you've proven to yourself that you can improve your thoughts, you know you can keep going! Remember, it's not about how fast you're climbing—this isn't a race. It's just you and yourself, moving forward.

Write your own ladder here, or maybe you need many ladders for different areas of your life. Also, it is a big help to look back at what your previous thoughts were. You will be amazed at how far you have come!

☆ _____ !!! ☺ _____ ☆ _____Celebrate the better place you are in_!!!!!!!!

⇧

_____ Keep going Up!

⇧

_____ Go up here next

⇧

_____ Start here

_____

_____

_____

_____

_____

_____

_____

_____

CHOOSE YOUR FEELINGS BY CHOOSING YOUR THOUGHTS

Sometimes when you are going through life, you might feel trapped by your emotions, especially when you're experiencing a strong negative one. It can seem like it's impossible to feel any other way. But I'm happy to tell you that you can change your emotions. Your emotions are completely influenced by your thoughts, and you have control over your thoughts. Don't make the mistake of believing that your thoughts just happen automatically in response to what's going on. You are free to choose how you think about any situation. You're not controlled by the things that happen to you—you control how you think about those things, and in turn, how you feel.

_____

_____

_____

_____

_____

_____

_____

_____

Have you ever heard the phrase, "I woke up on the wrong side of the bed"? That always confused me because, as far as I know, beds only have a left side and a right side—not a right side and a wrong side! What people really mean is that they believe bad things have been happening to them ever since they got up. And often, when they say this, they assume their entire day is going to be bad because of that "wrong side" excuse. But here's the thing—you have more control over your day than you might think. Suppose something happens in the morning that you're not happy about. You have choices:

- Hang your head and stay mad, convinced you're going to have a bad day.
- Tell yourself that it's not so bad, and think there must be something good in it, too.
- Decide it's too early in the morning for so much overthinking.
- Move on and start looking for the good things that are going to happen today.

The great thing about the last choice is that when you look for good things, you find them. There are always good things to be found: bright sunshine, rain to keep the plants alive, friends happy to see you, new things to learn, your favorite shirt clean again… When you look for the good, awesome things start showing up everywhere to make you happy.

_____

_____

_____

_____

_____

_____

Examples:

Sometimes, this is easier than other times. For example, if your younger sibling is talking smack about how slow you are in a game of Mario Kart (because that's what younger siblings do), it's easy to brush it off. But when a "friend" at school tells you you're bad at sports because you tripped over a tree root while running to catch a Frisbee, that can be harder to shake off. Even though these situations seem totally different, you can choose to handle them the same way.

Take your sibling and Mario Kart, for instance—you get to choose your thoughts and feelings about it. You could think, "He's just excited that he's winning right now, especially since I beat him the last 17 times." Or, "She's thrilled she's finally getting better, like her big sister." Then, your feelings are light, and you continue having fun. But you could also choose other thoughts like, "I'm really losing my skill here—how could I let this happen?" or "I have to be the best every single time and can't let anyone else win!" With those thoughts, you might feel disappointment and anxiety, and suddenly think you need to practice Mario Kart for an hour every day.

I hope this example shows you how you can choose your feelings instead of being trapped by them. The Mario Kart situation doesn't change—your thoughts about it are what create your feelings.

Now let's look at the Frisbee situation. Again, you can choose how you want to feel by choosing the thoughts you have about it. For example, there's the classic, "Could I be any less coordinated?" or "Wow, now everyone knows how clumsy I am." Those thoughts probably won't lead to happy feelings. ☹

But you can choose different thoughts: "I bet that'll be the most epic wipeout of the day!" or "I fell, but I did a great job getting back up." Again, the event doesn't change, but you have the power to choose your thoughts—and everything else that comes with them. And hey, if there were a blooper reel for school sports, you'd probably win top spot!

_____

_____

_____

_____

_____

_____

_____

_____

_____

_____

_____

_____

Sometimes, you can't change the events happening around you, but you can always choose how you think about them—and your feelings will follow.

Now, it's time to practice this together. Think of a situation, describe it, and then come up with different thoughts and how each one would make you feel.

Situation:

_____

_____

_____

_____

Thought 1

_____

_____

_____

_____

Feeling you chose

_____

_____

_____

_____

Thought 2

_____

_____

_____

_____

Feeling you chose

_____

_____

_____

_____

_____

_____

_____

_____

_____

DECIDE YOUR WORTH
AND STICK WITH IT

Now that we have been chatting about loving yourself, talking to yourself in a nice way, and ways you can get your thoughts to a higher level another important thing is to evaluate what things that you are going to hold on to no matter what. This means deciding what things you will choose to focus on and believe no matter what changes in your life. This is the best time to do that since we have already talked about loving and talking positively to ourselves,

_____

_____

_____

_____

_____

_____

_____

_____

_____

When you can direct your thoughts, you can choose the things that you focus on. Think about what you want to focus on, not just on what your friends are choosing to focus on. Other people have different priorities than you do, and they might bring those to you, thinking that you think it is just as important as they do. If your friend tells you that you need to grow your hair out to be more beautiful, that is one possible thing to focus on, but maybe you think the chic, short style is better. If your teacher tells you if you strengthen your math skills you could join the math team, that is another possible thing to focus on. At this point you have different things that people are bringing things to your attention, so you get to choose what you want to prioritize. Keep in mind that just because people are telling you something they think is important, does not mean that it has to be equally important to you.

There will be a lot of people in the world who think you need to prioritize the same things that they do. That is usually because that is the way they view the world, so they assume everyone else thinks the same things. Just because someone is insisting that you pay attention to something does not mean you have to care about it as much as they do. Maybe you choose to grow your hair out because you like that, or maybe you want to keep rocking your trendy short haircut. Maybe you choose to start doing extra math practice, or maybe you choose to focus on your sports tournament until the championship is over. When you are able to direct your thoughts, you can choose the things that you focus on.

You can use this same approach if people are saying things about you or to you. Just because they said it doesn't make it true or mean that you must accept it about yourself. Just because your friend says that you are not cool because you want to run track instead of playing lacrosse does not mean that you are required to care as much about lacrosse as they do. It is always your choice. If someone says you are not cool that does not make that statement true, or make it something you need to worry about. They could just as easily have said that you are an alien who lives on the moon.

Just because they said it does not make it true or make it something you must worry about. You might think one of those is hurtful and one of them is just silly, but there are both just someone else's opinion and don't have to be your problem. They are only your problem if you choose to freak out about them.

We already talked about how your thoughts influence your emotions, so that is a major reason you might want to be extra careful about what thoughts you let in. Just because someone else it fixated on it does not mean it is important for you to choose those thoughts as well.

What are the thoughts you want to believe and prioritize right now?

1.

2.

3.

What are some examples of thoughts that other people are prioritizing right now that you are choosing to prioritize less than them?

1.

2.

3.

_____

_____

_____

MAKE IT A HABIT TO NOTICE AND CELEBRATE THE WONDERFUL THINGS IN LIFE

The way you approach your life and events around you will have a huge impact on your happiness. You can choose to see bad things and fixate on them, or you can choose to focus on the good things that are all around you. You are free to choose any thoughts you want to have about a situation. Your thoughts are not controlled by the things that happen to you or around you. Instead, you are in control of what you think about a situation, and then the way you feel.

For example, let's say you see your friend sitting in front of you on the school bus. You ask him how he is doing and if he finished that super difficult math homework. You see him nod his head, but he doesn't say anything or even turn to look at you. That is the situation. Now there are some different options for what you can think and how you will feel.

The first option is "Well, fine I didn't want to talk to you either." Then you feel mad that your friend is blowing you off.

The second option is "I wonder if he has his ear buds in and is just rocking out to music." You tap his shoulder and find out that he didn't hear you say anything, and he was nodding his head to the music.

In this situation there are at least a couple different ways you could choose to think about what happened. The first way resulted in some anger and possibly resentment that your friend was ignoring you. The second way was a simple adjustment and gave your friend the benefit of the doubt, not assuming that he would ignore you on purpose.

You can't always change the events going on around you, but you can always choose your thoughts, and by doing that you can change your feelings about them.

What are some events in your life right now that are making you feel trapped by your emotions?

1. _____

2. _____

How are you going to choose to think about them?

1. _____

2. _____

_____

_____

_____

_____

_____

_____

_____

_____

_____

_____

_____

_____

_____

_____

_____

_____

_____

_____

You always want to examine if the way you are feeling is the way you want to be feeling. Are you feeling like you are rocking at life right now? Are you feeling discouraged? If it's not how you want to be feeling, then change it. You don't have to walk around feeling sorry for yourself. If you do, realize that it is your choice to feel that way.

Your feelings follow your thoughts so if you direct your thoughts, and your feelings will follow. Your actions then follow your feelings. If you are feeling mad you might be unkind to someone else. If you are feeling happy you might give someone a compliment and make them feel better too. Always try to be aware of how powerful your thoughts can be.

What are some of your thoughts and how can you make them more powerful?

_____

_____

_____

_____

_____

What feelings and actions could follow those powerful thoughts?

_____

_____

_____

_____

_____

SNAP OUT OF THE CRAZY CYCLE

You can choose to break free from the crazy cycle. If you're not familiar with it, the crazy cycle is like the opposite of a fun amusement park ride. Sure, you go around and around, but instead of being exciting, it just gets darker and gloomier. For example, the other day I stubbed my toe. Along with the pain and hopping around, my mind immediately started serving up unhelpful thoughts like, "I'm such a klutz!" and "I probably looked ridiculous running into the chair that was clearly right in front of me." These thoughts weren't kind or helpful, and they definitely didn't make me feel better. But then the cycle kicked in. My mind kept spiraling, adding more negative thoughts: "I've never been very coordinated." That led to, "I wasn't great at sports because I'm not coordinated or talented." Then it snowballed into, "That's why I don't like exercising—I never get it right." And, deeper down the rabbit hole, "That's why I have such a hard time staying healthy and getting fit."

If you think that's overly dramatic for just bumping my toe, you'd be right. The crazy cycle gets the best of me sometimes, and it makes everything feel overwhelmingly negative. It becomes hard to remind myself of the good things in my life, even though I know they're still there. It's like sliding down a dark tunnel and having no idea how I ended up at the bottom.

What helps me is stopping myself before I go too far. One way I do this is by monitoring my feelings. If I notice I'm feeling unusually negative, I stop and check my thoughts before I spiral further down the cycle. I figure out what's causing those negative feelings.

Once you've identified the thoughts dragging you down, you can choose to let them go. Replace them with new, empowering thoughts—and make the switch!

You have some good positive thoughts you chose last chapter, and you can bring in some new ones too and write them here.

1. _____

2. _____

3. _____

Then go for it! Maybe you'll listen to your favorite song to pump yourself up. Or perhaps you'll try the ladder method mentioned earlier. Maybe you'll go exercise to "shake off" the negative thoughts and feelings swirling in your head. You know what works best for you.

List a couple of options that will work for you:

1. _____

2. _____

3. _____

Even when I find myself stuck on negative things, I remind myself that I can choose to shift my focus and see the positive, even if it's something small. And here's the best part: the things we focus on tend to expand, making your ability to choose what to focus on your secret weapon.

The crazy cycle might get the best of us at times, but we can still choose to focus on the positive, even when it feels difficult.

_____

_____

_____

_____

_____

_____

_____

_____

_____

_____

_____

_____

_____

_____

_____

CUT YOURSELF A BREAK LIKE A BEAR

In our day-to-day lives, there are moments when things don't go perfectly. During times when you feel confused or overwhelmed, remember to pause and focus on your breathing. Even if you can't step away for alone time, the physical act of relaxed breathing sends signals to your brain that it doesn't need to stay in crisis mode. The more you use this technique, the more your brain will recognize it as a chance to reset. If you do have a few minutes to yourself, take that time to just focus on your breathing. Don't try to solve everything—just focus on your next breath in and your next breath out.

As you practice this, you'll start to feel better physically, which creates space for your brain to feel better emotionally. You don't need to fully understand the exact biology of how physical actions affect your emotions—just like you don't need to be an electrician to turn on a light switch. It works regardless. So, take the win and be grateful.

Sometimes, when you do this, your subconscious brain will come up with the answer—or at least the first step. Or maybe it will remind you that you're stressing over something that's hours, days, or even weeks away, and you can loosen up right now. If you don't need to solve the problem this very second, give your brain the gift of holding off on the panic. Sometimes, your brain works best at its own pace and might surprise you with the solution later, when you're not even thinking about it.

If you have the chance for a longer break, don't hesitate to take it. Your body and mind thrive on moments of rest, leaving you feeling re-energized afterward. Taking a break—or giving yourself a timeout—isn't a sign of weakness; it's part of the process of growing stronger. If the idea of "taking a break" feels silly or doesn't resonate, call it something else. Call it hibernation. 😊 Grizzly bears are among the strongest animals in the world, and they're also champion nappers. That's great company to keep!

What are some quick things you can do to signal that it's time for a break?

1. _____

2. _____

3. _____

_____

_____

_____

_____

_____

_____

_____

_____

A common joke for anyone who's ever contacted technical support about a computer problem is that the first question they'll ask is, "Have you tried turning it off and back on again?" It's funny because it's true—many problems can be fixed by simply stopping and starting over. Similarly, if you're using the internet for research or other tasks, you've probably noticed that having too many programs or tabs open slows everything down. Even computers struggle to function well when overloaded. And guess what? Our personal "computers"—our brains—work the same way.

Taking a step back, pausing, and starting over can help clear mental clutter. This kind of reset allows us to prioritize tasks, regain focus, and approach challenges with a fresh perspective. Just like rebooting a computer resolves glitches and improves performance, giving ourselves a break can enhance our cognitive function and creativity.

Sometimes, your body will give you physical signals that you need a reset. Maybe you feel sleepy or notice a tightness in your chest when things start to feel tense. Perhaps you're sweating or just feel "off" in a way you can't quite pinpoint. These are cues that it's time for a quick mental reset. You might step into the bathroom to run cold water over your hands or face. If you can't leave your current space, take a few deep breaths and think about something enjoyable, like your next weekend adventure.

What strategies could work for you to signal your brain that it's time for a reset?

1. _____

2. _____

3. _____

BE THANKFUL

One of the most powerful ways to improve your life is by practicing gratitude. Even if you feel like there's not much to be grateful for, it's there if you take the time to look. When you actively look for things to appreciate, you'll find them. Of course, it's not always easy to feel grateful. Sometimes, I find myself in situations where my gratitude sounds more like, "Well, I'm glad these three-year-old shoes still fit, because my dog chewed up the other ones and I'm already late!" or "I'm definitely grateful my rain jacket doesn't have a hole in it." Starting small is okay; with practice, you'll work your way up to being grateful for bigger things—like the rain itself, even when it messes up your weekend plans.

Even the smallest amount of gratitude can shift your mood. Changing how you feel for just five minutes can lead to finding more things to appreciate in the next five minutes—and before you know it, you've had a pretty great day.

_____

_____

_____

_____

_____

_____

Gratitude is one of your greatest superpowers. You might think it doesn't matter to feel grateful for things you already have, or that saying "thank you" is just something your parents taught you to be polite. But genuinely feeling thankful has huge benefits. Gratitude makes you happier, and when you're happy, people notice—they enjoy being around you. Even the universe picks up on your positive vibes, bringing more good things your way. Think of the universe like a giant matching game: when you're feeling down, it matches that energy with things that keep you feeling bad. But when you're grateful—even for something small, like your favorite purple pen—it matches that with more reasons to feel happy. The universe is a bit like Netflix, suggesting experiences based on what you're "watching." Focus on gratitude, and you'll attract more things to be grateful for.

I know it might sound strange to say you can just "choose" your feelings, but hear me out. Look around. Do you have shoes on your feet? Clothes on your body? They might not be perfect, but they're protecting you, keeping your feet safe, and preventing those embarrassing "underwear in public" dreams from coming true.

It might feel silly at first, but like anything else, gratitude gets easier with practice. When you make gratitude a habit, people might start thinking you're just really "lucky." But you'll know the truth: good things come to you because you appreciate them, and the universe notices. Everyone loves being appreciated!

Start right now. Look around. You're holding an awesome book, probably sitting in a comfy chair or lying in bed. You've got clothes on, a roof over your head… the list goes on. Don't be afraid to get creative! For example, I have a dog whose tongue is hilariously too big for his mouth—it's always hanging out, and it makes me laugh. My neighbor across the street loves decorating for every holiday, so I always know what's coming next just by stepping outside!

Practice gratitude every day. Sometimes, the amazing things will pop up on their own and blow you away. Other times, you'll need to really look for them. And I mean really search—like when you lose your phone, it's on silent, and no one is around to call it. Look that hard, and you'll find them.

Things to be thankful for.

1. _____

2. _____

3. _____

4. _____

5. _____

6. _____

7. _____

_____

_____

_____

_____

_____

_____

BE KIND AND SPREAD PEACE

Once you've started practicing some of the ideas in this book, take a moment to look around and think about how you can share your peace and gratitude with others. Sometimes, the best reason to be kind is simply because you can. When you bring your positivity to a situation, it's a blessing for others—and for yourself. Win-win!

Picture this: you have a secret peace spray bottle, and whenever you're near someone, they're unknowingly misted with a soft glow of calm. Or maybe you have tiny fans that blow a soothing breeze, helping others feel a little more relaxed whenever you're around. You might wonder why you'd spend time imagining spritzers or fans, but here's the thing—when your mind is filled with peaceful thoughts, your body naturally reflects that energy. You can choose your vibe, groove, aura, or whatever you want to call it. When you're in your peaceful, calm zone, you attract more of that energy and share it with the people around you. You never know what's happening in someone else's life, so even the smallest bit of positivity you offer might turn their entire day around.

_____

_____

_____

_____

_____

Remember, you don't know what others are going through. Offer grace and cut them some slack. Maybe they got yelled at this morning, are stressed about a quiz grade, or have a sick dog needing attention in the middle of the night. You can't control anyone else's life, and most of the time, you don't even know half of what they're dealing with. Don't judge or blame people when you don't know the full story—and since you're not a mind reader, you'll never know the whole story. So, choose kindness whenever possible.

If your life is going great right now, recognize that you can be a bright light for someone else, even when they say something mean. Maybe they're reacting to being bullied on the bus or getting chewed out at home before leaving for school. You don't know why they're being rude. Would it be nice if they weren't? Of course. But you can't control their actions; you can only control how you respond. You could choose to be mean back, thinking, "They started it!" Or you could choose to let it go. And if it helps, sing "Let It Go" from *Frozen* in your head—or don't. 😊

Keep spreading your peaceful vibe with that imaginary spray bottle. Just because you don't have an awesome "Be Kind" rainbow shirt like mine doesn't mean you can forget that kindness is one of your superpowers. Think of creative ways to spread peace—without actually spraying people, because that might not go over well. Maybe you could write a quick note of encouragement and leave it where someone will find it. Or hand out free high fives. Whatever fits your style, spread that peace everywhere you go.

Ways I can spread peace:

1. _____

2. _____

3. _____

4. _____

5. _____

6. _____

_____

_____

_____

_____

_____

_____

_____

_____

_____

Printed in the United States
by Baker & Taylor Publisher Services